Berenice

Berenice

Jean Racine

A translation by
R.C. Knight,

completed and edited by
H.T. Barnwell

Durham Academic Press
Edinburgh – Cambridge – Durham – USA

First published in 1999 by
Durham Academic Press Ltd
1 Hutton Close
South Church
Bishop Auckland
Durham

ISBN 900838 10 9

Berenice

Typeset in Baskerville 12/15
by Carnegie Publishing, Carnegie House, Chatsworth Road, Lancaster
Printed and bound by Antony Rowe Ltd, Chippenham

Contents

Prefatory Note

In 1982, the Cambridge University Press published Roy Knight's translation of Jean Racine's *Andromache, Iphigenia, Phaedra* and *Athaliah*, under the title of *Four Greek Plays*. The translator had hoped to continue this work with most of the playwright's other tragedies, and had indeed made considerable progress with it when he was overtaken by illness. The translation of *Berenice* was virtually complete, but the manuscript showed a small number of lacunae and a much larger number of alternative versions. It was thought, however, by Miss Margaret Tillett, with whom Roy Knight had discussed his translation, and whose suggestions were noted in the manuscript, that it might be possible to complete the work. As one whose first research had been supervised many years ago by Professor Knight, and who had subsequently ploughed the same research field, and collaborated with him, I was asked if I would undertake the task. Although fully aware of its delicacy and of my own limitations, I willingly did so as a small tribute to a fine scholar and teacher, and a friend for over half a century.

I have used such judgement as I possess in choosing between alternative renderings and in filling the lacunae, in the hope that what I have done is not too inconsistent with the remainder of the translation. The editorial matter is also mine apart from a few passages in the introduction which, appropriately modified, are borrowed from that to *Four Greek Plays*. I have tried to follow the spirit and intention of that volume, but acknowledge that any deficiencies and failures are my own. It is hoped that *Berenice* will give pleasure to the readers of *Four Greek Plays* and introduce others, whose French may be imperfect or non-existent, to the consummate art of a great tragic poet.

My thanks go to Mrs Glenys Bridges not only for her word-processing skills, but also for her watchful eye on my errors; and to Mr Anthony Phillips and Mrs Mary Denton.

H.T.B.

Introduction

For many, *Berenice* is the summit, at least from a technical point of view, of its author's tragic art; others regard it as undramatic because it is plotless, and elegiac rather than theatrical. Racine's insistence in his Preface on what he calls the simplicity of the play does not for him preclude theatricality: on the contrary the 'violence of the passions' and the heroine's struggle to accept the inevitability of her parting from Titus make the subject eminently suitable for dramatic treatment. However, for those who come to Racine's tragedies, and to *Berenice* in particular, from the background of English drama (and that, especially, of Shakespeare and his contemporaries) such claims may be puzzling. Even Dryden's adoption of the staging conventions of the French theatre in his *All for Love* (1678), a play on a theme similar to that of *Berenice* – like Racine in his Preface, he in his prologue suggests similarities also with Virgil's account of Aeneas's parting from Dido – does not by any means lead him to write such a simple play, for he acknowledges in his Preface that his tragedy is largely inspired by *Antony and Cleopatra*. The traditions and conventions of the French stage in Racine's time call, therefore, for brief explanation.*

---

* Passages within single quotation marks are reproduced, by kind permission of Cambridge University Press, from the General Introduction of Jean Racine, *Four Greek Plays*, translated by R.C. Knight, Cambridge University Press, 1982.

'While Racine was writing, an old and influential literary tradition was at its last gasp – that part of Renaissance doctrine which had taught that all the arts could find themselves, and rise again, only by imitating the works and methods of classical antiquity; with freedom and originality, but in the spirit of admirers and learners. Instead, a new spirit was growing, of self-confidence and self-congratulation before the evidence of recent advances in scientific knowledge, technology, and also literature and art; a complacency far from groundless, but aided by a fading awareness of what had been the greatness of Greece and Rome. The "Quarrel of the Ancients and Moderns" was a long succession of petty cavils and critical skirmishes: of the two pitched battles, in which the Ancients were defeated by their own pedantry and the ignorance of their opponents, one came late in Racine's life and the other after his death. He took his place among the Ancients, but inconspicuously, and no doubt never realised how much of a Modern he was in the nature of things.

'For the drama in which he excelled (born of Renaissance imitations of the Latin tragedies of Seneca, with an admixture of the drama of love and adventure, inspired by the modern novel, and in France called tragi-comedy) is modern, and has few of the features or of the beauties of Attic tragedy. It has great merits of its own, which redeem what the English reader tends to see as considerable constraints. Thus, rigid (but not quite complete) unity of tone forbad comic relief or colloquial language (though not simplicity and directness) to intrude into a fairly sustained nobility of tragic vocabulary and expression. An exalted sense of decorum, which would have seemed exaggerated in any less hierarchical society, excluded the sight of bloodshed, violence and crowd scenes, but led back at the same time to the realisation that drama resides much less in pageantry or any other visual appeal, than in great crises of emotion, clashes of wills (or ideas), crucial dilemmas and decisions. The cramping effect of the famous Unities of Time, Place and Action has often been overstressed. The first two were born of a misconceived devotion to "verisimilitude", taken to mean a hundred per cent illusion of reality in performance instead of the credibility of the story-line; their effect was to eliminate all plots but those which could be played out in a single place and a single burst of activity, based on a situation which had to be explained by, often, a great deal of reference to the past. But they were powerful aids to concentration and intensity; so, even more, was the strict Unity of Action, under which sub-plots were not excluded, but had to be very closely integrated. At the same time a new awareness of "plot" developed the arts of climax and suspense.

'Such was the dramatic form into which Racine infused a poetry and a sense of tragedy (we are still struggling to define those terms) which made his dozen years of writing the apogee of this utterly French genre. (He wrote nine tragedies for the Paris stage, 1664-77, then two in retirement, 1689 and 1691.) Meanwhile in his prefaces, which contain all the ideas he ever expressed on the art of tragedy, he wrote from the beginning as if all the merits of his plays had been due to a return to the examples of Sophocles and Euripides, and the lessons of Aristotle.'

However, Sophocles and Euripides had known nothing of the love-interest Racine's century would not do without, or of the conventions under which it was forced to operate. Subjects drawn from Greek mythology or Roman history, the sources which his public recognized as providing the Aristotelian 'traditional stories' on which tragedy should be based, were necessarily interpreted in modern terms, the action being radically modified in such a way as to appeal to seventeenth-century French taste. This meant, with varying emphases, the superimposition on the source material of a love-plot of the kind found in tragi-comedy and novels and a conflict of political interests. These elements exist in all Racine's secular plays and they inevitably result in some complexity in the creation of the plot and dramatic action.

His trumpeting of the simplicity of *Berenice* must be set against the background of his rivalry with Pierre Corneille, his senior by thirty-three years and for long the dominant figure in the French tragic theatre. The complexity of Corneille's later tragedies and his persistence in portraying characters of extraordinary heroic virtue (though much modified from his earlier manner) were no longer much to the taste of the audiences of the 1660s and 1670s, who looked above all for romantic love-plots and for the subtle, often over-subtle, psychological and emotional dilemmas which animate them. Corneille himself did not escape their influence and, in particular, made it one feature of his 'heroic comedy', *Tite et Bérénice*, first performed on 28 November 1670, exactly a week after the first performance of Racine's play. The possibility of the two playwrights deliberately choosing to vie with each other, perhaps at the instigation of rival groups of supporters, in writing on the same episode of Roman history, has been the subject of much scholarly debate; but it need not detain us here. Suffice it to mention that in his Preface, published with *Berenice* in January 1671, Racine expressed evident satisfaction with the success of his tragedy. Corneille's much more complex play achieved a run of only twenty-one performances, acted before ever smaller audiences. Racine's was not without critics, but his extraordinarily simple drama of intense passionate love in conflict with and eventually defeated by political duty and necessity, and expressed in the most appealing poetic language, brought him instant acclaim and a triumph over his ageing rival. From his first tragedy, *La Thébaïde* (1664), to *Berenice* Racine had progressively simplified the construction of his plays. He could go no further in that direction after 1670, and subsequently was less concerned with simplicity.

His truncated quotation, at the head of his Preface, from Suetonius's *Life of Titus* refers to the separation (AD 79), reluctant on both sides, of the Emperor from the Palestinian princess, Berenice; but that statement could not alone provide him with a dramatic theme in which conflict was essential: the most it could give him was material for the 'elegy' which has so often been taken to be the real nature of the play, and the word does admittedly describe many of the wistful and melancholy passages of its poetry. *Berenice* is, however, both a real drama and a real tragedy. Making use of suggestions from historians other than Suetonius and from works of seventeenth-century fiction, Racine fills out *invitus invitam* by putting at the centre of his tragedy the incompatibility of the Orientals' despotic concept of monarchy with the Romans' devotion to the supremacy of Senate and People. Titus knows throughout that he has the inescapable duty to respect and uphold that supremacy and the tradition of hostility to emperors' marriages to foreign princesses. In love with such a princess, he is engaged in the inner drama and conflict of having to send her away whilst wishing, in his love, to avoid causing her, in her love, grief and pain. For her part, she knows (her confidant Phenice, reminds her of reality, as Paulinus reminds Titus of his duty) that Rome would not accept her marriage to the Emperor; but she deludes herself into believing that he is free, on his accession after the death of his father, Vespasian, to do as he wishes. She interprets his silences and apparent coolness as loss of love for her, a radical misunderstanding based on the presence (not historical) of Titus's former ally in the East, and hers, Antiochus, who is also in love with her.

Although Titus has sometimes been seen, in spite of its title, as the central character of the play, Berenice's tragedy is its subject: she has to come, painfully, through a dramatic reversal of her expectations to recognition of the truth that she resists: Titus does love her, but cannot marry her. (Antiochus has to realize that, although Berenice respects him, she does not love him and will not marry him.) Racine's conception of a passionate, virginal heroine and a sympathetic, tender hero forms the psychological basis of his play. Their dignity and, eventually, their stoical resignation, together with the great political issues in which they are involved, lift their separation above the realm of domestic drama into that of tragedy. The insurmountable obstacles to the fulfilment of love lie in the political realities which both Titus and his confidant survey; but the obstacles to Titus's revelation of the bitter truth to Berenice and to her acceptance of it lie within themselves, and in overcoming them they achieve the moral grandeur inherent in tragic drama, a grandeur whose cost is suffering, the destruction of the most cherished hopes of all three principal characters. But the integrity of the Roman Empire, threatened by those hopes, is preserved.

The political situation sets Racine's drama in aspects of the historical reality as he found it in Suetonius, Tacitus, Herodian and Josephus. Until near the end, his Berenice has only an illusory grasp of that reality which he evokes, allusively, in the most poetic manner, in the implicit contrast between the clamorous, populous city of Rome and the desolate Orient to whose emptiness (empty above all of love) his heroine (and Antiochus) must return. How little is said of the Orient, and how largely Roman history and tradition feature in the utterances of Titus and Paulinus! In reality, Berenice was a powerless little princess, never queen of Palestine. (No more was Antiochus king of Commagene, a territory in north-east Syria already incorporated in the Roman Empire by Vespasian.) But Racine follows Suetonius in conferring the title on her and, finally, endows her with a corresponding moral nobility in her dignified resolve, in spite of the loss of all she holds dear, to go on living and so to dissuade Titus and Antiochus from the suicide to which they are tempted. All three go their separate ways into their bleak future.

The drama created by Racine is nowhere to be found in the ancient historians, and the characters bear little resemblance to their historical counterparts. They are to a large extent idealized through suggestions probably found in works of fiction or fictionalized history. Titus is already the virtuous man he was in real history later to become; Berenice is chaste, and virtuous too, and a good moral influence on him, quite the contrary of the reality. The harrowing grief of Berenice comes in part from that of Dido, both in the *Aeneid* (Book IV) and in the Dido plays of Scudéry (1637) and Boisrobert (1643). Berenice's single-minded devotion to her love and her disdain for ambition probably derive from Scudéry's portrait in *Les Femmes illustres* (1655) and Magnon's in his play *Tite* (1660). The comradeship between Titus and Antiochus is adumbrated in a play on a different subject, Le Vert's *Aricidie* (1646). Other suggestions may come from accounts of Titus and Berenice in Coëffeteau's *Histoire romaine* (1621) and Le Moyne's *Galerie des Femmes fortes* (1640-43). The unhistorical role of Antiochus probably came from an unfinished novel, *Bérénice*, by Segrais (1651): it enables Racine to dramatize the Suetonian account by introducing both an element of jealousy and the concomitant misunderstandings which persist until the middle of the very last act of his play. All these and other suggestions allow Racine to make something out of nothing, as he puts it in his Preface, and to enrich the bare statements of Suetonius with the complexity needed to make them dramatic. The much-vaunted simplicity is, after all, only relative. His tragedy is a modern play with a poetic aura of antiquity, and his heroine is the only Berenice most Frenchmen know. (The same might be said of Andromache and Phaedra.)

The conflicts between and within the characters are given visual expression in Racine's exploitation of the Unity of Place and the single set in which the play is acted. He defines the place with exceptional precision as a closet situated between the apartments of Titus and Berenice, a private refuge from the politicians and crowds of Rome. There, the characters can exchange confidences. But the off-stage presence of politicians and crowds is palpable and, as references in the text reveal, menacing. The intertwined initials of Emperor and Queen within the garlands which decorate this room represent ironically the union to which they aspire but which cannot be achieved. Their movements through the doorways on either side give visual expression to their struggle to avoid separation and, finally, to accept it; and, for example, the conflict within Titus at the end of Act IV, between yielding to duty by meeting the representatives of the Senate in his apartment (stage right), and saving Berenice from suicide by entering hers (stage left), is symbolized by his hesitation between the two doorways and eventually passing through his own. (A third doorway, in the backdrop, leads outside and, symbolically, away from the city.

Berenice presumably passes through it at the end.) Exits and entrances, indicated in the French convention as changes of scene, and the use of emissaries (Antiochus, Arbaces, Rutilus) are all likewise significant in the dramatization of the characters' emotions. Racine exploits also the theatrical tradition of giving to the main protagonists confidants (Paulinus, Phenice, Arbaces) who allow those to whom they are attached to express their innermost feelings without having always to resort to soliloquy, and often prompt consciences or recall realities and duties. The final separation of the three principal characters and their enlightenment (the Greek *anagnorisis*) are rendered the more poignant by their sole meeting as a group occurring in the very last scene.

On matters of language and versification, the translator must be allowed to speak for himself. He writes of 'the principal beauty of Racine' as 'the sheer music of his verse'. 'It depends on vowels and consonants, speech rhythms, metrical and intonation patterns, which are French and not English. Here has always been the barrier to recognition of Racine in English-speaking countries. Perhaps the barrier is insurmountable. Each translator does what he can to find some sort of equivalents. Here I will explain what I have tried to do, rather than why I could not do better.

'The metrical form itself cannot be reproduced: French and English are too different in their ways of applying stress and therefore creating rhythm. Only by the number of syllables (twelve) does Shelley's alexandrine in the *Skylark* ode, or Byron's in *Childe Harold*, resemble the French alexandrine. So, like most or all other English translators, I take our traditional line for serious verse, the decasyllable; but I do not attempt rhyme, for one thing because English is poor in rhymes and it would be too difficult to reconcile rhyme with tolerable fidelity to

sense, but also because the couplets of Dryden, Racine's con-
temporary, to say nothing of those of Pope, are not perhaps
more often endstopt or more neatly balanced than Racine's,
but being shorter they are more evidently so. But my blank
verse is less irregular than much of Shakespeare's, is never
mixed with prose, and has no incomplete lines. For all specific
effects – pauses, phrasing, climax, *accelerando* and *rallentando* –
I try to find equivalents.'

Racine made use of the fairly restricted gamut of images
common to his contemporaries: 'laurels or trophies (for military
glory), blood (with perpetual play between the two connota-
tions of "slaughter" and "dynasty"); in the domain of
love-making, the post-Petrachan metaphors of flames, wounds
and bonds; and the preference for metonymies (heart, hand,
arm, eyes) over personal nouns and pronouns. Clichés all, or
in the process of becoming clichés, for these were simply the
successful turns of expression favoured, because of their known
power to communicate the sense of poetry, until the moment
when over-familiarity caused distaste; but while they were as
widely current as they were in Racine's day, that moment had
clearly not come . . .

'The vocabulary of Racine's tragedies is restricted to some
2,000 words, some of which, because of the relative scarcity
of available synonyms, have taken on great richness of mean-
ing. In a more copious language I could not imitate this,
though I have respected his use of theme-words as much as I
could, together with his avoidance of low or inelegant turns
of speech, and some of the dead metaphors of lovers' language
which I have described as clichés – but not those too obviously
dead; by trying to find out how we today might express the
same concepts I hoped to recover some of the freshness that
they must have had once.

'I have respected some of Racine's linguistic conventions – for instance that by which all high-born characters address each other normally as *Seigneur* or *Madame*, or occasionally, for a little more familiarity (strange as it may seem) as *Prince* or *Princesse*. Other such conventions were hard to reproduce – those adjectives (used as nouns) of hyperbolical denunciation which English no longer possesses, *cruel, inhumain, barbare, perfide, infidèle, ingrat* (in either gender) . . .'

A brief note on proper names is called for. They are rendered in the normal forms in English of the Latin originals. In Racine's text, however, Antiochus's confidant is *Arsace*. The translator must, rightly, have felt that the three sibilants of *Arsaces* would be anything but euphonious; the solution adopted, *Arbaces*, was probably suggested by the name of Mithridate's confidant, *Arbate*, in Racine's play of 1673. All the proper names in *Berenice*, coming into English through French, should be pronounced as though naturalized in our language, that is, as they were universally pronounced before the introduction in our schools, early in this century, of the presumably authentic pronunciation of Latin, and as names such as Caesar, Titus, Cicero are always enunciated. The matter is of some importance for the music of the vowels, in particular, in this translation, and for the placing of stress. Using the symbols adopted in the *Concise Oxford Dictionary*, the characters' names should be pronounced thus [*see overleaf*]:

Tī′tŭs

Bĕrĕnī′cē (see)

Antī′ŏchŭs (k)

Paulī′nŭs

Arbā′cēs (sees)

Phĕnī′cē (see)

Rū′tĭlŭs

Cŏmmăgē′nē (jeenee)

Studies on Racine in English

G. Brereton, *Racine: a Critical Biography* (Cassell, 1951; 2nd edn, Methuen, 1973).

E. Vinaver, *Racine et la poésie tragique* (1951; 2nd edn, 1963), translated by P.M. Jones as *Racine and Poetic Tragedy* (Manchester University Press, 1955).

J.C. Lapp, *Aspects of Racinian Tragedy* (University of Toronto Press, 1955; 2nd edn, 1964).

K.E. Wheatley, *Racine and English Classicism* (University of Texas Press, 1956).

B. Weinberg, *The Art of Jean Racine* (University of Chicago Press, 1963).

O. de Mourgues, *Racine; or, The Triumph of Relevance* (Cambridge University Press, 1967).

R.C. Knight (ed.), *Racine* (Modern Judgements) (Macmillan, 1969). Fourteen critical essays in English.

M. Turnell, *Jean Racine Dramatist* (Hamish Hamilton, 1972).

G. Brereton, *French Tragic Drama in the Sixteenth and Seventeenth Centuries* (Methuen, 1973).

P. Butler, *Racine: a Study* (Heinemann, 1974).

P.J. Yarrow, *Racine* (Plays and Playwrights) (Blackwell, 1978).

J. Lough, *Seventeenth-Century French Drama: the Background* (Oxford: Clarendon Press, 1979).

N.K. Drown, *Jean Racine: Meditations on his Poetic Art* (no place, 1982).

D. Maskell, *Racine: A Theatrical Reading* (Oxford, Clarendon Press, 1991).

M. Hawcroft, *Word as Action: Racine, Rhetoric and Theatrical Language* (Oxford, Clarendon Press, 1992).

R. Parish, *Racine: the limits of tragedy* (Biblio 17, 1993).

H. Phillips. *Racine: Language and Theatre* (University of Durham Press, 1994).

Specifically on Berenice

Racine: *Bérénice*, ed. C.L. Walton (Clarendon French Series) (Oxford University Press, 1965). Contains a valuable introduction.

G. Pocock, *Corneille and Racine: Problems of Tragic Form* (Cambridge University Press, 1973). Chapter 14.

H.T. Barnwell, *The Tragic Drama of Corneille and Racine* (Oxford, Clarendon Press, 1982). Chapter 2.

J.J. Supple, *Racine: Bérénice* (Critical Guides to French Texts) (Grant and Cutler, 1986). A comprehensive short introduction.

Preface

*Titus reginam Berenicem, cui etiam nuptias pollicitus
ferebatur, statim ab urbe dimisit invitus invitam.*[1]

That is to say that 'Titus, who passionately loved Queen
Berenice and who, it was believed, had promised to marry
her, sent her away from Rome, against his wishes and hers,
during the first days of his reign.' This action is renowned in
history, and I found it very suitable for the theatre, on account
of the violence of the passions it might arouse. Indeed, nothing
can be found in all poetry more touching than Virgil's account
of the separation of Aeneas and Dido.[2] And who can doubt
that what could provide enough material for a whole canto of
a heroic poem, whose action lasts several days, could fail to
suffice as the subject of a tragedy whose duration should not
exceed a few hours? True, Berenice is not in my play driven
to suicide, as is Dido, because Berenice, not being bound to
Titus by the ultimate pledges which bind Dido to Aeneas, she
is not under the same constraint to withdraw from life.[3] That
excepted, her last farewell to Titus and her struggle to part
from him is not the least tragic aspect of the play; and I go
so far as to say that it intensifies in the hearts of the spectators
the emotion already aroused by what precedes it. Tragedy
does not necessarily demand bloodshed and death; it needs
no more than an action endowed with grandeur, characters
of exalted status, the arousal of the passions and, throughout,

that stately sadness which is the source of all one's pleasure in tragedy.

I thought that all these elements were to be found in my subject. But what pleased me even more was that I found it extremely simple. I had for long wished to discover whether I could create a tragedy with the simplicity of action so much appreciated by the ancients. For it is one of the first precepts they have bequeathed to us. 'Let whatever you do,' says Horace, 'be always simple and unified.'[4] They admired Sophocles' *Ajax* which is nothing more than Ajax killing himself out of remorse for his madness on being refused the arms of Achilles. They admired *Philoctetes* whose entire subject is Ulysses' subterfuge in acquiring Hercules' arrows. Even *Oedipus*, although full of discoveries,[5] has less subject-matter than the simplest tragedy of our times.[6] Finally, we see that those who approve of Terence, rightly setting him above all comic poets for the elegance of his style and the verisimilitude of his characterisation, yet confess that Plautus is greatly superior to him in the simplicity of most of his subjects. And it was doubtless this simplicity which attracted all the praise the ancients heaped on Plautus. How much simpler still was Menander, since Terence was obliged to take two of his comedies to make one of his own![7]

And it is not to be thought that this rule is founded merely on the whim of those who made it. Only verisimilitude can arouse the tragic emotions.[8] And what verisimilitude is there in a multiplicity of things happening in one day which could scarcely occur in the course of several weeks? Some think that this simplicity betokens a lack of inventiveness. It does not occur to them to think that on the contrary inventiveness consists purely in making something out of nothing, and that a multitude of incidents has always been the recourse of poets who felt in their genius neither sufficient verbal resources nor enough imaginative power to keep their spectators' attention through five acts by a simple action, sustained by violent passions, noble emotions and elegant expression. I am far from believing that all these things are to be found in my work; but at the same time I cannot believe that the public are ungrateful to me for producing a tragedy which has been honoured by such abundant tears and whose thirtieth performance was as well attended as the first.[9]

It is not that some people have not criticised me for that same simplicity which I had so assiduously tried to achieve. In their opinion, a tragedy with so little plot could not conform with the rules of drama. I enquired whether they were complaining that they had found my play boring. I was told that none of them was bored, that they were often touched by it, and that they would go and see it again with pleasure. What more do they want? I beg them to think of themselves highly enough not to believe that a play which they find moving and which gives them pleasure can be radically at variance with the rules. The principal rule is to please and to arouse the emotions.[10] The sole purpose of all the others is to satisfy this first one. But all these rules require detailed examination with which I advise them not to concern themselves. They have more important things to attend to. Let them rely upon our efforts to explain the difficulties of the *Poetics* of Aristotle; let them keep for themselves the pleasure of weeping and being moved to pity; and let me say what a musician said to Philip, King of Macedon, when he asserted that a certain song was not composed according to the rules: 'God forbid, my lord, that you should ever be so unfortunate as to be more competent than I in such matters!'

That is all I have to say to those people whom I shall always be proud to please. For, as for the lampoon written against me, I think that my readers will gladly excuse me from replying to it.[11] And what should I say to a man who has no thoughts and who is incapable of putting order into what he thinks? He speaks of protasis as though he understood the word, and demands that this first of the four parts of tragedy be always nearest to the last, which is the catastrophe.[12] He complains that too great a knowledge of the rules prevents his enjoyment of plays. Certainly, to judge by his treatise, no complaint was ever so ill founded. He has obviously never read Sophocles whom he quite wrongly praises for a great *multiplicity of incidents*, and has never read the *Poetics* other than in a few prefaces to tragedies. But I forgive him his ignorance of the rules of drama, since fortunately for the public he does not apply himself to that kind of writing. What I do not forgive is his imperfect knowledge of the rules for making good jokes, since he wishes his every word to be a joke. Does he expect to delight many well-bred people with '*Alas*! scattered like small change', those 'school-mistressy rules', and many other base conceits which he will find condemned by all good writers if he ever dabbles in reading them?[13]

All these criticisms are the portion of four or five hapless little authors who have themselves never succeeded in arousing the curiosity of the public. They are for ever on the look-out for some successful work so as to attack it. Not out of jealousy. For why should they be jealous? They do it in the hope that one will take the trouble to reply to them and drag them out of the obscurity in which their own works would have left them all their lives.

Berenice

Dramatis personae

Titus, emperor of Rome

Berenice, queen of Palestine

Antiochus, king of Commagene

Paulinus, confidant of Titus

Arbaces, confidant of Antiochus

Phenice, confidant of Berenice

Rutilus, a Roman

Court of Titus

The scene is at Rome, in a private room between the apartment of Titus and that of Berenice.

Act I

Scene 1

Antiochus, Arbaces

Antiochus	Here we can stop. For it is clear, Arbaces,
	You never saw these stately halls before.
	This little study, rich and so sequestered,
	Has often heard the secret thoughts of Titus
	When sometimes he plays truant from his
	<div align="right">court</div>
	And comes to lay his love before the Queen.
	This door leads off into his own apartment,
	And that one to the Queen's. Go to her:
	Tell her that though I would not trouble her
	I have to beg a private audience.

10

Arbaces	You, my lord, trouble her? The loyal friend,
	Generous and devoted in her service;
	You, Antiochus, the man who loved her once,
	A king among the greatest kings of Orient?
	What if she is to be the bride of Titus?
	Does that exalt her far above your state?

Antiochus	Just go and ask, never mind these questions;
	Find out if I can see her soon, alone.

[Exit Arbaces]

<h2 style="text-align:center">Scene 2</h2>

Antiochus		So, can you do it now, Antiochus?
[solus]	20	Look in her eyes and tell her that you love
		her?
		Why, now I am trembling, and dread this
		hour
		As deeply as I ever longed for it.
		Long ago Berenice dashed my hopes
		And told me not to speak of love again.
		Nor have I, these five years; and till today
		The lover hid behind the mask of friend.
		Am I to think she'll show me more
		compassion
		Now Titus marries her and raises her
		To such a height? Was this the time to choose
	30	For telling her that I am still in love?
		What can I gain by disobedience?
		No; rather go without offending her
		If go I must; go now, without a word,
		Out of her sight to die there or forget.
		— What? suffer all this pain, and she not
		know?
		Shed all these tears, and never dare to show
		them?

Fear to offend her, though I know I've lost
              her?
— Sweet Queen, and why then should you
              take offence?
Do I demand that you renounce the Empire?
40 I ask for nothing; or, at most, to tell you
That after waiting long to see if Titus
Meet with some obstacle to cross his love,
Now he may please himself and speak of
              marriage.
After five years of wasted hopes and ardours,
I go, still faithful although I hope no more.
I go, a paragon of constancy.
She might show pity and forget her pride.
Come what may, I must speak: it must come
              out.
And what has he to lose, who is resigned
50 Never again to look upon her face?

[Arbaces returns]

Scene 3

Antiochus   May I go in, Arbaces?

Arbaces   I have seen her,
My lord, though I could hardly force my way
Between the swelling tides of worshippers
That her new fortune draws behind her steps.
Titus has finished with the week of mourning
In honour of Vespasian his father;

The lover turns towards his love again;
Indeed, if I may credit what I hear,
Before tonight the happy Berenice
60 May trade the name of Queen for that of
Empress.

Antiochus   Alas!

Arbaces   But why, my lord, should this distress
you?

Antiochus   It means I cannot see her by herself.

Arbaces   Ah, but you will, my lord. The Queen has
heard
What you desire, and told me with a nod
That she would grant it. She is waiting now,
I think, to snatch some opportunity
For throwing off her uninvited court.

Antiochus   Ah! very good. And those important orders
I left with you? Have they been carried out?

Arbaces   70 Yes, at all points, my lord. In Ostia
Ships have been fitted out with every care
And only wait the word to put to sea.
But who is ordered back to Commagene?

Antiochus   We leave at once after my audience.

Arbaces   Who is leaving?

Antiochus		I am.
Arbaces		You?
Antiochus		I leave this place

And leave the city, never to return.

Arbaces I am amazed of course, and well I may be.
— What! After all the time Queen Berenice
Has drawn you from your kingdom to her
side,
80 Three years' attendance on her here in
Rome?
Now that the Queen's assured of her desires,
Calls on you to attend the solemn rites,
And now that the love of Titus sheds on her
A lustre that must fall in part on you —

Antiochus Arbaces, leave her to her happy lot
And drop a subject that I find distressing.

Arbaces I think I see, my lord; those dignities
Have closed her eyes to all that you have
done;
And friendship unrewarded turns to hate.

Antiochus 90 Never, Arbaces, did I hate her less.

Arbaces Well then, is the new Emperor too full
Of his own dignity to know his friends?
Do you foresee some cooling in his friendship?
And are you leaving Rome because of this?

Antiochus	Titus has shown no change in his affection.
	I have no cause . . .
Arbaces	And why then must you
	leave?
	Why should you do yourself this injury?
	The Gods have put a friend upon the throne,
	A prince who saw each of the feats of arms

Titus has shown no change in his affection.
I have no cause . . .

And why then must you
leave?
Why should you do yourself this injury?
The Gods have put a friend upon the throne,
A prince who saw each of the feats of arms
100 With which you followed him to death or
glory,
The soldier you enabled to reduce
The Jewish rebels in their stubborn stand;
He can recall that great, that dreadful day
Which tipped the balance of a weary siege
When, tranquil in his triple ring of walls,
The enemy watched our useless strokes with
scorn;
The ponderous ram spent all its blows in vain;
And you snatched up a ladder, you alone,
To carry death in their own walls to them.
110 That was the day that might have been your
last:
Titus embraced you prostrate in my arms,
And all the conquering army mourned you
dead.
Now is the time, my lord, for you to reap
Some profit from the blood they saw you
shed.
If you desire your own domains so much
That where you do not rule you cannot live
Must you return with nothing in your hands?
Stay here, till Caesar sends you back again

In glory, loaded with those lofty titles
120 That Roman friendship can bestow on kings.
Will nothing change your resolution then?
You do not answer?

Antiochus   What am I to say?
I am waiting for a word with Berenice.

Arbaces   And then my lord?

Antiochus   Her lot will settle mine.

Arbaces   How so?

Antiochus   I want to hear from her about
Her marriage. If she says what they all say,
That she is destined for the imperial throne,
If Titus has decided, and they marry
I go.

Arbaces   Why do you fear that marriage so?

Antiochus 130 You shall hear all the rest when we're at sea.

Arbaces   Your words have filled me with dismay, my
                                          lord.

Antiochus   The Queen is here! Goodbye. Do what I said.

[Enter Berenice and Phenice. Exit Arbaces]

Scene 4

Berenice   At last, I have escaped the new-found friends
That fortune brings me, and the tedious joy
And useless babble of their salutations
To meet a friend whose talk is from the heart.
I will be frank — I thought you were remiss
And blamed you for neglecting me already.
How could this be, I thought, Antiochus
140   Whose constant care the whole of Rome has
                         seen
And all the Orient, who never failed me
But followed me in all my chequered fortunes
With equal zeal, and never-daunted heart?
And now at last that Heaven seems to promise
Honours that you shall share as well as I,
Has this Antiochus gone into hiding
And left me coping with a crowd of strangers?

Antiochus   So it is true, my lady, what they say,
That you will see your wedding-day at last?

Berenice   150   Well, I have had misgivings; these last days
Have seen me shed some tears; and the long
                         week
That Titus forced his court to spend in
                       mourning
Has told upon his love, even alone,
Even with me; the eager thirst was gone
With which he had hung long days upon my
                       eyes.
All that he gave me was a gruff farewell.

Judge what I felt; have I not told you often
I love him for himself, and if he lost
His princely rank, his name and all his titles,
160 Should see his heart and choose him for his
virtues?

Antiochus   But he has shown his early love again?

Berenice   You saw last night with how much circum-
stance
The Senate carried out the son's desire
By raising up his father to the Gods.
This pious office satisfies his duty
And he is free at last to be a lover.
Why, even now without a word to me
He has convoked the Senate and is there
Stretching the boundaries of Palestine
170 And adding to it all Arabia,
All Syria too; and if his friends speak true,
If I may trust what he has sworn so often
He will give these lands to Berenice
To crown these titles with the name of
Empress.
And he is coming here to tell me so.

Antiochus   So I am here to say farewell forever.

Berenice   What do you mean? Farewell? How can you
say it?
You are not yourself, Prince, your looks are
strange.

Antiochus	My lady, I must go.
Berenice	Well you must say
	180 What makes you . . . ?
Antiochus	I should have gone
[aside]	and never seen her.
Berenice	What do you fear? Speak out. For I must know;
	What is the secret, Prince, of your departure?
Antiochus	At least remember you have made me speak
	And I shall never speak to you again.
	If, in your height of glory and of power,
	You still remember where your life began,
	My lady, you remember it was I
	Who first fell victim to your loveliness.
	I loved. I was accepted by Agrippa,
	190 Your brother, and he spoke for me. Perhaps
	The heart I proffered would have been accepted;
	But Titus came, saw you, and won your love.
	He came in all the splendour of a man
	Who held the Roman vengeance in his hands.
	He turned Judaea pale, and poor Antiochus
	Soon learnt that he was numbered with the losers.
	I knew it when I heard your pitiless sentence
	Forbidding me to speak of love again.
	I fought, with the weak weapons of my tears.

200 And with looks and sighs that would not let
                                    you go;
    But in the end your cruelty prevailed
    And made me choose to leave you or be
                                    dumb.
    But I had to promise, had to swear an oath,
    But even so, I dare confess it now,
    When you extorted that iniquitous promise
    My heart was swearing love for evermore.

Berenice   How dare you tell me that?

Antiochus   I've kept my word
    Five years, my lady, and I'll keep it longer.
    — I made myself the comrade of my rival,
210 Hoping to drop my blood instead of tears
    Or that at least a thousand warlike feats
    Would bear my name to you, if not my voice.
    Heaven seemed to send the closure of my
                                    pains:
    You mourned my death — alas, I did not die.
    Danger was unavailing, vain my hopes —
    Titus outdid my power with his valour.
    I owe this tribute to a hero's worth:
    Though destined to be ruler of the world,
    Though loved by all, even though loved of
                                    you,
220 He seemed to bare his breast to every blow
    While I, disdained, despairing, sick of life
    Seemed not his rival but his follower.
    — I see his praise is music in your ears;
    I see you listen less unwillingly

~ 13 ~

To the unhappy story that I tell
And let me have my say for Titus' sake. —
But then at last the long hard siege was over,
The rebels crushed, that pale and bloodied
                    remnant
Of fire, of famine, of internal strife,
230 Their walls left buried underneath their ashes.
You went with Titus and appeared in Rome,
And all the Orient was desolate.
Meanwhile I loitered long in Caesarea,
Enchanted realm where you had been my
                    queen.
I searched to trace your footsteps, and I wept.
At length, when I could bear my pain no
                    longer,
I let despair drive me to Italy —
And the last blow of fate. Titus embraced me
And brought me to your side; you saw in me
240 Only the friend that I had claimed to be,
And shared with me the secrets of your hearts.
But still I cherished one consoling hope:
Rome, and Vespasian, opposed your love,
And Titus, tired of struggling, might give way.
Vespasian died; Titus is free to marry.
I should have gone at once: I planned to wait
Just long enough to see his reign begin.
— My day is over, and your hour has come.
You will not miss my figure in the crowds
250 That come to join their pleasure to your joy;
While I, who only have my tears to add,
Unwearying victim of a fruitless love,
Happy, in all my woes, to be allowed

To tell their history to you, their source,
Now go my way, loving you more than ever.

Berenice   My lord, I never thought that on a day
Which is to see my union with Titus
Any man living would be bold enough
To come and speak to me about his love.
260 For friendship's sake I pass the matter over:
I can forget the insult of your words;
More, I am sorry that you have to go.
It gives me pain to hear you say farewell —
For heaven knows I needed only you
To see me taste the honours it has sent me.
With all the world I held you in respect;
Titus made much of you; and I thought as he
did.
Often I found it bliss beyond compare
To speak to Titus in another such.

Antiochus 270 And that is why I go, because of Titus,
To avoid those dialogues I never share,
To escape from Titus, the name that haunts
me,
The name that is for ever on your lips.
What shall I say? To escape those careless
eyes
That never saw me, who was always there.
Farewell, I go, your picture in my heart,
To nurse my love and to await my death.
And never fear that unregarding grief
Will fill the world with echoes of my
sorrows —

₂₈₀ Only when someone tells you I have died
Will you remember that I ever lived.
Farewell.

[Exit Antiochus]

Scene 5

Phenice   So long a constancy
Surely deserved a better end than this.
I pity him; don't you?

Berenice   That quick departure
Has given me some pain, I do confess.

Phenice   I would have kept him back.

Berenice   I, keep him back?
My duty's to forget all that he said.
Should I have pity on his senseless dreams?

Phenice   Titus has not declared his purpose yet;
₂₉₀ And Rome will not accept you willingly.
The law of Rome is harsh, it frightens me.
Rome hates kings: Berenice is a queen.

Berenice   Those fears are past, Phenice; Titus loves
                                    me.
The power is his. He only has to speak
To see the Senate ply me with his tributes

And Romans crown his statues with their
                wreaths.
— You saw last night, Phenice, its splendour;
Such majesty must still be in your eyes:
The night in flames, the torches and the
                bonfires,
300 Eagles and legions, lictors, populace;
The huddled Kings, Consuls and Senators,
Transfigured by the gleams my lover shed,
Purple and gold, ennobled by his glory.
Those laurels, telling of his victories still;
The eager gaze of crowds from far and
                wide
Fixed there on Titus, and on him alone;
That noble bearing, that appealing grace,
Ah, how much loyalty, what devotion
Glowed in each heart that pledged its service
                there!
310 Tell me; if he had come into the world
Without a name, without a family,
Would not the crowds he passes in the street
Say as I say, "There goes a prince of men"?
— But memory must not carry me away;
All Rome is hastening at this very hour
To pray for Titus, and with offerings
To celebrate the dawning of his day.
Why do we wait? We too must go and
                pray,
Offering gifts for Heaven's high protection
320 And blessings as he enters on his reign.
Then I shall come, not waiting, un-
                announced,

To seek him out, and find a time to say
All that two lovers happy in their love
Have had to stifle in their hearts so long.

[Exeunt]

Act II

Scene 1

Titus, Paulinus, Courtiers

Titus   Has someone told the King of Commagene
      To come and see me?

Paulinus   I tried the Queen's
               apartment;
      He had been there, but he had gone away.
      I sent word of your orders after him.

Titus   Good. And Queen Berenice, what of her?

Paulinus 330 The Queen, in gratitude for all your bounties,
      Is offering prayer for your prosperity.
      I saw her leave, my lord.

Titus   She is too good,
      Poor soul!

Paulinus   But why this sorrow in your
               voice?

Half of the Orient, almost, will be hers.
You pity her?

Titus   A word with you, Paulinus.

[Signs to the others to leave. They retire.]

Scene 2

Well now: Rome still is guessing at my plans,
And asking what will happen to the Queen,
Paulinus; her most private thoughts and mine
Are now the gossip of the universe.
340 It is high time for me to speak my mind;
But tell me now what people say of us.
Speak out: what do you hear?

Paulinus   Nothing but
                              praise,
Praise of your goodness, and her charms, my
                              lord.

Titus   What of my aspirations to her hand?
              Do they expect to see them realised?

Paulinus   Do what you will: love her or let her go.
              You'll always find the court is ready to
                              applaud.

Titus   Yes, that obsequious, lying court; I know it,
              I've seen it praise the wickedness of Nero

350 And celebrate his ravings on its knees.
I shall not ask those sycophants to judge me,
Paulinus; I prefer a nobler audience:
I want to hear the inmost thoughts of men
Out of your mouth; for that was what you
        promised.
Fear, and too much respect, have blocked the
        way
For any breath of blame to come to me.
Therefore I asked you for your eyes and ears;
That was the price at which I set my
        friendship;
You were to tell me what was in men's hearts,
360 To tear away the veil of flattery
And let me see the truth. So tell me now:
Can Berenice hope for anything?
Will she find Rome complaisant or severe?
Must I suppose such beauty and such grace
Would be resented, set on the Caesars'
        throne?

Paulinus   No doubt of it, my lord. It may be prejudice.
It may be principle: Rome does not want her.
They know she is enchanting; and such hands
Seem to demand the governance of the world;
370 Her heart, they say, beats like a Roman heart;
She has every virtue; but she is a queen.
Rome, by a law that never can be altered,
Will have no alien blood to mix with hers,
But disavows and brands with bastardy
All issue of a different union.

Yes, and you know, when she cast out her
                                        kings,
That name, so noble once and so august,
Drew to itself such hate and execration
That though she shows her Caesars loyalty
380 That hate, last memory of an ancient pride,
Lives in her heart, when liberty is dead.
Julius, the first to master Rome by arms
And in their clamour drown the voice of law,
Loved Cleopatra, but would not confess it,
And let her languish in the Orient.
Mark Antony, whose passion knew no bounds,
Forgot for her his honour and his country
Till Rome sent out in wrath to punish him
And take him at her knees, and would not rest
390 Till she had overthrown the two of them.
Since then Caligula, my lord, and Nero,
Those monsters I can scarcely bear to name,
Devouring beasts concealed in human shape
Who trampled over every law of Rome,
Respected only this, and never dared
To risk a union that she abhorred.
— You told me to be frank above all else:
We have seen the brother of the freedman
                                        Pallas,
Felix, still marked with sores of Claudius'
                                        fetters,
400 Marry two queens; and if, my lord, I must
Obey you to the end in what I say
The two were of the kin of Berenice.
So can you think that you could bring a
                                        queen

Into the Caesars' bed without offence,
While queens of Orient accept in theirs
A slave, as soon as he can lose his chains?
— That is how Romans view a love like
                              yours.
And who knows if, before the day is gone,
The Senate, speaking for the Roman state,
410 Will not be here to say what I have said
And bring all Rome to fall before your feet
And beg a choice worthy of her, and you?
But you have time to think what you will say.

Titus   But what a love they want me to forgo!

Paulinus   It will be hard to break, I see that well.

Titus   Harder by far than you will ever guess,
Paulinus; I have needed every day
To go and see her, love her, make her love
                              me.
More than that — I will tell you all the
                              truth —
420 Because of her I've often thanked the Gods
Who picked my father back in Idumaea
To pacify the Orient and the legions,
Then, after raising up the world in conflict,
Left mangled Rome between his guiltless
                              hands —
I even longed to fill my father's place —
Yes, I, Paulinus, who so cheerfully
Would have resigned my life, had Heaven
                              allowed,

To lengthen his, for it had been my hope
(How little lovers know what's good for them!)
430 To see her raised on the imperial throne,
To recompense her fond and faithful heart,
And take my place kneeling among her
                              subjects.
So now, for all my love and all its spell,
After so many vows, so many tears,
Now that I have the power to pay my debt,
Now that I love her more than ever I did,
Now that a longed for marriage can fulfil
All that I've prayed and promised five long
                              years,
I have resolved — Gods, can I speak the
                              word?

Paulinus   440 You have resolved . . . ?

Titus   To let her go for
                              ever.
This is no sudden impulse of surrender:
If I have questioned you and heard you out
It was to let your loyal warnings work,
And put to death a love I could not kill.
The issue long was doubtful, and if now
I see myself follow the call of honour,
Believe me, to struggle free from so much love
Has cost me wounds which will not close
                              tomorrow.
I was a lover, and I loved in peace;
450 No weight of empire rested on my head;
I ruled my fate, accountable to none;

But once the Gods had called my father to
them,
And once my orphan hand had closed his
eyes,
My comfortable illusions fell away;
I felt the burden that was laid upon me;
No longer free to give my heart at will,
But forced, Paulinus, to renounce myself,
To know the choice of Heaven forbade my
love
And gave my days, however short they be,
460 In joyless bondage to the Roman world.
Rome wants to see how I shall turn about.
What shame for me, what augury for her
If I should overturn her rights at once
And build my happiness on shattered laws!
I had resolved this bitter sacrifice,
And thought how best to warn poor Berenice.
But where to start? How many times this week
Have I essayed to find the words to do it.
And at the outset, every time my tongue
470 Has frozen in my mouth and failed its office!
I hoped at least my grief and my distress
Would give some hint of what awaited us;
But no, she pities me and guesses nothing,
Offers her hand to wipe away my tears;
Nothing is further from her mind than this,
That all the love I owe to her must end.
At last, today I summoned up my will:
I will see her, Paulinus, I will speak.
I have called Antiochus to charge him with
480 This priceless treasure that I may not keep,

And Rome shall see her leave with him
                 tomorrow.
I shall tell her so myself upon the instant,
And I shall never speak to her again.

Paulinus   I looked for this from you: your love of glory
Has never failed to bring you victory.
Do not Judaea and her smoking walls
Still testify to that heroic fever?
And who could doubt your courage would
                 refuse
To bring to ruin all that you had done?
490 I knew the victor of so many fields
Would soon or late subdue his own desires.

Titus   But what a bitter thing, this vaunted glory!
How much more welcome to my wounded
                 heart
If life were all I had to pay for it!
Think of it — all my thirst for its allurements
Was first of all the gift of Berenice.
You know full well, not always was my name
Accompanied with all those terms of praise.
My youth was spent within the court of Nero
500 And those examples had corrupted me,
Paulinus, and the easy slope of pleasure.
Then, I loved her. What will a man not do
To please his mistress and to gain her love?
I spent my blood unstinting; none withstood
                 me.
Victories fell to me. But blood and wounds
Were not a worthy price to gain her favour.

I sought the miserable and made them happy.
I poured out charity without constraint,
Happy, and happier than you can think
510 When I could please her by the train I
                          brought
Of grateful hearts recruited by my gifts!
I owe her all I am, Paulinus. And for this
All she has made me falls back on her head.
She gave me glory, gave me character:
I tell her, "Go: we must not meet again."

Paulinus   Oh come, my lord, what of those lavish plans
To stretch her rule as far as the Euphrates,
Titles that took the Senate by surprise;
Do they accuse you of ingratitude?
520 Scores of new peoples will acclaim her queen.

Titus   And what is that to heal a grief like this?
I who know Berenice know too well
That all she ever hoped for was my heart.
I loved her, she loved me; and since that day,
— That glad, or tragic day, which shall I call
                          it? —
Loving, and living only for her love,
An alien in Rome, at court unknown,
She lives and asks only for this, Paulinus,
Some hour with me, the rest to wait.
530 And even if at times I am too late,
And pass the time when she expected me,
I find her bathed in tears, and it is long
Before my hand can dry them. Everything —
All that is strongest in the bonds of love.

Murmured reproaches, raptures ever new,
Artless desire to please, constant misgivings,
Goodness, glory, virtue and beauty, all are
                    hers.
These last five years I've seen her every day
And every day seems to me like the first.
540 I must not think of it. Come on, good friend;
Thought only dulls the edge of my resolve.
What news, great Gods, have I to give her
                    now!
Come on. Once more, I must not think of it.
I see my duty, I shall follow it,
And never ask if I can live beyond it.

[Enter Rutilus]

Scene 3

Rutilus   My lord, the Queen is here and asks to see
                              you.

Titus   The Queen? — Paulinus!

Paulinus   What! retreat
                              already?
                 Recall your noble purposes, my lord.
                 Now is the time.

Titus   Very well, let her come.

[Enter Berenice and Phenice]

Scene 4

Berenice   550   Do not be angry if my eagerness
Has made me interrupt a conference:
At such a moment when your court can speak
Of nothing but these gifts of yours to me,
Can it be right, my lord, that I alone
Should not attempt to show some gratitude?
But, my lord — for I know this trusty friend
Knows all the deepest secret of our
                       thoughts —
Your mourning's over, nothing holds you
                       back.
Alone at last, you did not come to me.
560   They tell me of another crown that you are
                       giving,
And yet I may not hear you tell me so.
So, please, my lord, more peace and less
                       parade!
Can you show love only in the Senate?
Oh, Titus — for I will not use these styles
Of servile fear — does love need ceremony?
Has it no present but a crown to give?
What makes you think I hanker to be great?
A heart like mine asks nothing but a word,
A look, a sigh. Come oftener to see me
570   And bring me nothing. Have the claims of
                       empire
Sole claim upon your life? A week has gone,
And is there nothing you could say to me?
Think what a word would do to soothe my
                       spirits!

But tell me, when I came just now, was I
The subject of your talk, or did you name me,
Or did you even think of me at all?

Titus   Never doubt it, my lady. Heaven is my
                                        witness,
My thoughts are always full of Berenice.
Not time nor distance, hear me swear again,
580 Can rob you of this true adoring heart.

Berenice   What, you can swear undying passion for me,
And swear it in these cold and rigid terms?
Why should you need to call upon the Gods?
As if without an oath I could not trust you?
Indeed, my lord, I do not disbelieve you.
A single sigh from you is all I need.

Titus   My lady . . .

Berenice   Yes, my lord? Can you not
                                        answer?
Will you not look at me? You seem disturbed.
Shall I see nothing but these wandering eyes?
590 Is it a father's death that still affects you?
Will nothing charm away that dark despair?

Titus   Ah! Would he were alive, my father, still!
How happy I could be!

Berenice   Those sentiments
Are proper to show you a loving son, my lord.
But you have wept enough, and it is time

To turn your thoughts to Rome, and to
                    yourself.
(I will not speak of claims that I could make.)
Time was, when Berenice could console you,
When you could find some comfort in my
                    words;
600 Have I not suffered persecution for you
And dried my tears in payment of one word?
You mourn a father — light and passing
                    sorrow!
And I — the memory still harrows me —
They tried to rob me of my only love;
And you know well the anguish I endure
If I should love you for one little hour;
I, who should die if ever I were forced —

Titus   My lady, stop! Why do you say such things,
And say them now? These words are far too
                    kind
610 For one so undeserving —

Berenice   How could you,
                    my lord,
Be undeserving? Must I think
That I perhaps have wearied you with
                    kindness?

Titus   Never, my lady, since you challenge me,
Has love burned stronger in this heart of
                    mine;
But . . .

Berenice	Yes, go on!
Titus	Ah!
Berenice	Speak.
Titus	Rome . . . and the Empire . . .
Berenice	Well?
Titus	Come out, Paulinus, for I cannot tell her.

[Exeunt Titus and Paulinus]

Scene 5

Berenice What, break away, and not a word to me!
Was it for this I tried so hard to see him?
What have I done? What does he want?
What is this silence?

Phenice 620 I seek in vain and cannot understand,
Like you. But is there nothing comes to mind
That could have turned the Emperor against
       you?
Try to reflect.

Berenice   I give you my assurance,
The more I try to look into the past
From our first meeting to this dire day,

The more I see my fault was too much love.
— But you heard all we said. Tell me the
                              worst;
Speak out. Did I say something to offend him?
What can I think? Did I cry down his presents
630 Too much? Or blame his mourning for his
                              father?
Or can it be he fears the hate of Rome?
Afraid perhaps to make a queen his wife?
It might be that . . . But no, for many a time
He has told me not to fear that cruel law;
Many and many a time. But I must know,
I cannot breathe in all this doubt and silence.
How could I love, Phenice, if I thought
That he had slighted me, or I had hurt him?
I must go after him. — But, now I think,
640 Perhaps I see what lay behind this trouble —
He must have heard reports of what has
                              passed,
And taken umbrage at Antiochus.
They tell me that he meant to see the King.
That must be it: there is no other cause,
And all this black mood that has disturbed
                              me so
Is nothing but a flicker of suspicion.
Oh, Titus, there is nothing here to boast of!
I only wish some rival could appear,
One with more might (if that were possible),
650 And seek to lay more sceptres at my feet
To win my love with every kind of power,
While you had nothing but yourself to give!
Then, then, my Titus, I could prove to you

What you are worth to me, how much I love
you.
One little word can still his fear, Phenice.
All is not lost. His heart can still be mine.
I had given up myself for lost too soon.
If Titus can be jealous, Titus loves!

[Exeunt]

Act III

Scene 1

Titus, Antiochus, Arbaces

Titus   What is this, Prince? You giving us the slip,
660 In all this hustle and this secrecy?
Would you not leave me even a farewell?
Are you escaping from an enemy?
What must I think? What must my people
                 think,
I, and the Court, and Rome, and all the
                 Empire?
We have been friends; or have I treated you
As one more king among a crowd of kings?
You shared my secrets, while my father lived,
And that was all I had to share with you;
Now I can do all that I ever wanted
670 You dodge the gifts that only sought to find
                 you,
And seem to think that I forget the past,
Gloating on nothing but my present greatness
Till all my friends appear so far away

That I have ceased to know and ceased to
               need them?
Why you, so eager to avoid my sight,
I need you, Prince, I need you more than
               ever.

Antiochus   Need me, my lord?

Titus   Yes, you.

Antiochus   From one so
               wretched
What can you need, my lord, but loyal
               wishes?

Titus   I have not forgotten how your feats of arms
    680 Lent half their lustre to my victories:
How many conquered prisoners Rome has
               seen
Wearing the fetters of Antiochus,
While now the Capitol displays to all
The spoils you wrested from Jerusalem.
I am not asking now for deeds of blood,
Simply your voice as an interpreter:
I know that Berenice has always found
In you her best and truest advocate
And trusts no other counsellor but you;
    690 You are as one with us in heart and soul —
So, in the name of this abiding friendship,
Make use, I beg you, of the power you have;
See her for me.

Antiochus	How can I see her now That I have taken leave of her for ever?
Titus	Speak to her once again on my behalf.
Antiochus	You speak to her, my lord. She worships you; And why deny yourself at such a time The joy of making her the sweet avowal That day by day she wants and longs to hear?
	700 There will be no resistance, that I promise. She said herself that you were coming here Only to ask her to accept your hand.
Titus	What joy if I could make her such an offer! What happiness if it were mine to make! This very day I looked to taste that rapture, And yet today, Prince, I must let her go.
Antiochus	Let her go! You, my lord?
Titus	Such is my doom. Titus and she can never hope to wed. Prince, you must go away with her tomorrow.
Antiochus	710 What do you tell me? Gods!
Titus	Accuse my station: I am so great that I am powerless. I give men crowns, or take them back again And cannot freely give away my heart. Rome, that hates kings from immemorial time,

Cannot receive a queen born in the purple;
A glorious throne, a line of royal forebears
Disgrace my love and outrage every heart.
Hers is the only hand I may not have —
The meanest choice I made would be
                              acclaimed,
720 And Rome would take as Empress happily
The least illustrious beauty she had reared.
Julius himself gave way before this pressure.
Unless the mob see Berenice go
Tomorrow, she will see them come to yell
To have her sent away: from that affront
My name, her honour, must be safeguarded.
Since yield we must, then be it to our glory.
This week, the silence of my lips and eyes
Should have prepared her for this bitter
                              sentence,
730 And even now she hovers feverishly,
Waiting for me to tell her my intent.
Have a pity on a helpless lover's pains.
Spare me the agony of telling her
Why I am tortured, why I cannot speak,
So that at last she lets me go. Let no one
Be witness of the tears that we must shed.
Take her my farewells; let her give you hers
And save us both the intolerable moment
That might undo the rest of our resolve.
740 If she can take it as a consolation
That in my heart she will be always queen,
Swear to her, Prince, that lonely in my Court,
An exile more than she, and till the grave,
Wishing the title only of her lover,

My reign will be a long-drawn banishment;
If the same Gods that will not let me love
Should foist on me the burden of long days,
You, who for friendship's sake have never left
                                            her,
Stand by her, Prince, do not abandon her
750 But be her escort to the Orient;
Make it a scene of triumph, not defeat.
That noble bond, let it become unending,
And let my name be often on your lips.
To draw your kingdoms closer to each other
Their common boundary shall be the
                                      Euphrates.
The Senate knows your name; it will confirm
With one accord, I know, what I have said.
I'll join Cilicia to your Commagene.
Farewell: stay ever close to my Princess,
760 My Queen, sole object of my heart's desire,
My only love until I breathe my last.

[Exit Titus]

Scene 2

Arbaces   And so you come into your just deserts.
                 And you shall sail, but sail with Berenice
                 No longer lost, but thrust into your arms.

Antiochus   Leave me alone, Arbaces; let me breathe.
                 In such a change I do not know myself.
                 Can Titus yield me all he ever loved?

Can I believe, ye Gods, what I have heard?
— If I believe it, will it bring me joy?

Arbaces   770 But what am I to make of it, my lord?
What is the new obstruction to your bliss?
Was it untrue, that story that you told me
Not long ago, after your last leave-taking
When, moved and shaken at your full
                    confession,
You came and told me what you'd dared to
                    say?
You fled before the marriage that you feared:
But there is none, so what disturbs you now?
Give yourself up to savouring your fortune!

Antiochus   Why yes, Arbaces: I must be her guide.
        780 We shall be long in talk with one another.
Her eyes may learn to rest on mine again,
Her heart may make comparison between
Titus' indifference and my constancy.
Here, I am nothing under Titus' shadow;
But though his glory fills the Orient, yet
She may perhaps see traces of my deeds.

Arbaces   All will be as you wish, my lord, be sure.

Antiochus   How eagerly we two delude ourselves!

Arbaces   But why delude?

Antiochus   What, do you think she'd
                    love me?

790 Would Berenice listen to my love?
Would Berenice speak to ease my pain?
Do you imagine, after this rejection,
Unmarked, unsought by all the world beside,
She would accept the tribute of my tears
Or condescend so far as to receive
What she could see as offices of love?

Arbaces Who better to console her fall than you?
Everything changes now for her, my lord:
She loses Titus.

Antiochus   True, and this reversal
800 Will bring me nothing but the new ordeal
Of learning by her tears how much she loves
him,
Of hearing her laments, and grieving with
them,
And, as a recompense for all my love,
Of watching tears that are not shed for me.

Arbaces Why will you dwell so long on all these
thoughts?
How can a noble heart show so much
weakness?
Open your eyes, my lord; reckon with me
How many causes force her to be yours.
Consider, now that Titus is not hers,
810 She cannot well refuse to marry you.

Antiochus Cannot refuse!

Arbaces	Give her a day or two
	To overcome her earliest floods of tears;
	Resentment, anger, all will speak for you,
	Titus removed, time passing, you at hand.
	She cannot bear the burden of three sceptres;
	She cannot keep your kingdoms˙separate:
	Reason, friendship, policy unite them.

Antiochus   Thank you, Arbaces, you have given me hope.
I welcome such a happy prophecy;
820 I'll go and do it. That was all he wanted.
I'll go to Berenice, do my errand,
And let her know Titus is leaving her.
— No, I will not. How could I think it?
Is it for me to do this cruel thing?
Pity or love, I cannot bear the thought.
Could I inform my dearest Berenice
That he is leaving her? Queen, who'd have
               thought
That you would ever hear a word like this?

Arbaces   Well, Titus bears the odium of it all.
830 And if you tell her, it is by his order.

Antiochus   I will not go. I will respect her grief;
Others will flock to tell her of her fate,
And is it not sufficient hurt for her
To hear from them what Titus means to do,
Without the cruel torment of being forced
To learn it from the rival she rejected?
No, no. I'll leave this place rather than tell her
And call undying hate upon my head.

Arbaces	Well, here she is, my lord; make up your mind.
Antiochus	840 Ah Gods!

[Enter Berenice and Phenice]

Scene 3

Berenice	Why, not yet gone, my lord!
Antiochus	I've disappointed you, and I am sorry. Of course you wanted Caesar; but his orders Were what detained me in this room today. I might be on the quay at Ostia Had he not forced me not to leave his court.
Berenice	You are not the only one. He will not see us.
Antiochus	He kept me back only to speak of you.
Berenice	Of me?
Antiochus	Indeed.
Berenice	And what may he have said?
Antiochus	Ask someone else; for anyone will tell you 850 Better than I.
Berenice	My lord, come —

Antiochus   Hold your anger.
Another might be glad to spread the story,
And tell it joyfully, triumphantly
To your impatient ear. But you know me,
How much I tremble for your peace of mind
More than my own, and choose to disobey
And rather see your anger than your pain.
Before the day is out you will approve.
Farewell, my lady.

Berenice   Prince, you must not go.
What words! — I cannot hide my disarray.
860 You see a Queen before you, crazed with
                                     suspense,
Death in her breast, and pleading for one
                                     word.
You fear, you say, to break my peace of mind.
But these refusals, far from sparing me,
Wake in me pain, and anger, yes, and hate.
If you care so much for my peace of mind,
If I, my lord, was ever dear to you,
Tell me the truth and free my mind from fear.
What did he say to you?

Antiochus   In the Gods' name —

Berenice   What, are you not afraid to disobey me?

Antiochus   870 If I should answer I should make you hate me.

Berenice   I tell you, answer me.

Antiochus	Do you mean to force me?
	You will forgive me, I repeat, my lady.
Berenice	Do as I say at once, Prince, or be sure
	You have made me hate you, now and always.
Antiochus	No, after that I cannot hold my peace.
	You order me, my lady, and I obey.
	But steel yourself: for what I have to tell you
	May be more painful than you dare to think.
	Your heart is known to me; you must expect
	880 That I shall stab where it will suffer most.
	Titus commands me —
Berenice	What?
Antiochus	I am to tell you
	That you and he must part for evermore.
Berenice	Part! He, from me? Titus from Berenice?
Antiochus	Yet it behoves me to be just to him.
	All torments that a fond and noble heart
	Can feel when every hope of love is gone
	I saw in his. I saw his tears of love;
	But what can all his love avail him now?
	A queen is hateful to the Roman state;
	890 So you must part. Your ship will sail to-morrow.
Berenice	We must part! Oh, Phenice!

Phenice	Oh, my lady!
	Now is the time to show a lofty courage.
	This blow is hard: it leaves you thunderstruck.
Berenice	So many oaths, and now he lets me go!
	Titus, who swore — I never shall believe it.
	He will not leave me, honour will not let him.
	He has not done this: it is a calumny,
	A trick designed to break the bond between
	us.
	Titus loves me! Titus would never cause my
	death!
900	I'll see him, I'll go at once to ask him.
[to Phenice]	Come on.
Antiochus	What, do you think I could — ?
Berenice	It's what you wished. No, I do not believe
	you.
	How can I think it true? But true or false,
	See that you never cross my path again.
[to Phenice]	Stay with me. I need you. Ah, Phenice!
	You see how hard I try to cheat myself.

[Exeunt Berenice and Phenice]

Scene 4

Antiochus	But did I hear her right? Did she say that?
	That I must never cross her path again?
	As if I should! I who was on my way

~ 46 ~

910 When Titus made me stop against my will?
Of course I'll go. On with our plans, Arbaces!
She's tried to hurt me, but it's what I want.
You saw me hesitant, distraught, unsettled,
Loving and forced to leave, jealous and
                                        despairing;
And now, Arbaces, after what she said,
It may be I shall go without a pang.

Arbaces   You must not go, my lord, less now than ever.

Antiochus   What, stay to be the butt of her displeasure!
To take the blame for Titus' turning back!
920 To let her punish me for what he's done!
What is it but an insult, an injustice,
To tell me to my face she disbelieves me,
That Titus loves her and I played her false —
How can she? Charge me with this
                                        monstrous crime!
And at the moment, at the very moment
When to console her I depicted him,
My rival, full of grief and full of love
And constancy — more than he is perhaps!

Arbaces   Why let this weigh upon your mind, my lord?
930 Let but the gush of passion spend itself
And in a month, even a week, it's gone.
Just wait.

Antiochus   No, I will not, Arbaces!
I might be melted if I watched her tears.
My peace, and my good name, tell me to go.

~ 47 ~

Come away. Let it be so far from her
That for long years I never hear her name.
But there is time before the daylight fades:
I'm going to my palace. There I'll wait
While you find out how she has stood the
blow.
940 Be quick: we must not sail until we're sure.

[Exeunt]

Act IV

Scene 1

Berenice [sola]

Berenice
Phenice does not come. O laggard hours
That will not match the haste of my desire!
While here I chafe and pine, but cannot rise:
To rest is torment and I cannot stir.
Phenice does not come; dire forebodings
Press on my heart with every creeping
moment:
There can have been no answer she could
bring;
Titus has played me false, he will not see her;
He will not see me, will not face my fury.

[Enter Phenice]

Scene 2

950 What news, Phenice? Have you seen the
Emperor?

What did he say? And will he come?

Phenice   I saw him;
I told him of the tempest in your heart;
I saw him shedding tears he could not hide —

Berenice   But is he coming?

Phenice   Yes, he surely is;
But will you let him see you as you are?
Be calm, my lady, and collect yourself.
Let me replace those veils that you have lost
And comb away those locks before your
                                             eyes;
Let me restore the ravages of your tears.

Berenice   960 Let be, let be, Phenice; he shall see
What he has done to me. This finery,
These foolish toys, what do I care for them
If all my constancy, my weeping — weeping?
My certain death — if these will not recall
                                             him?
Why, what can any art of yours avail,
Or these poor charms, which mean no more
                                             to him?

Phenice   Why will you dwell on charges that are
                                             false?
— But I hear steps: it is the Emperor.
Come back, escape their prying eyes,
                                             withdraw

970 And let him come and find you in your
rooms.

[Exeunt Berenice and Phenice]

Scene 3

[Enter Titus, Paulinus and courtiers]

Titus   Paulinus, go and reassure the Queen,
I'll see her, but I need to be alone.
All of you, leave me.

[Exeunt courtiers]

Paulinus   How I fear this contest!
[aside]   Gods, save his honour, save the State's from
shame!
— I have to see the Queen.

[Exit Paulinus]

Scene 4

Titus   Well, Titus, now,
What have you come to do? Are you
prepared?
Your mistress waits for you. Your farewell
words,

Have you composed them? Are you sure you
          mean them?
Is there enough of cruelty in you?
980 For in the battle you have come to fight
Firmness will not suffice: you must be brutal.
Can I endure the pleadings of those eyes
That know so well the pathways to my heart?
Those potent eyes, so irresistible,
Fastened on mine, unman me with their tears,
Shall I remember what my duty preaches?
Can I declare, "We must not meet again"?
Can I transfix a heart that loves so well?
And why? What makes me do it? Only I.
990 Rome after all has not expressed her will.
No yelling crowds have come to ring these
          walls.
Is the State tottering on the brink of ruin?
Is this the only sacrifice to save it?
No: all is quiet. Only I in fear
Bring forward evils I could brush away.
And who shall say that Rome will not relent
At the Queen's virtues, and adopt her
          Roman?
What if Rome's will should ratify my choice?
No; once more no; for I have been too hasty.
1000 Let Rome set in the balance against her laws
Those tears, that love, that long fidelity;
Rome will be on our side. — Titus, wake up.
What air is this? And are these not the walls
Where hate of kings is sucked with mother's
          milk
And not to be expelled by love or fear?

Your Queen was doomed when Rome
                    abolished kings.
Did you not hear the sentence at your birth?
Later, when Berenice joined you here,
Did you not hear the mutterings of Rome?
1010 How often must you hear them? Palterer!
Go and make love, and let the Empire be!
Run to the world's end, hide, run and make
                    room
For someone worthier to fill a throne than
                    you.
Are these the lofty dreams of glorious deeds
That were to grave my name in memory?
One week I have been Caesar; and so far
What have I done for Honour? What for love?
How can I answer for these precious days?
Where is the Age of Gold I seemed to
                    promise?
1020 Have I done any good? Dried any tears?
Earned any thanks for acts of mine?
Have I rolled back the threat of any evil?
I cannot know how long I have to live,
And of these days, so ardently desired,
Spendthrift, how many have I tossed away!
I dare not wait. The voice of Honour speaks.
Only one bond —

[Enter Berenice]

~ 53 ~

Scene 5

Berenice	I tell you, let me go!
[to her	You do no good to try and hold me back.
women	I have to see him. — Is it you, my lord?
within]	1030 So, is it true Titus sends me away?
	We are to part? And he has said we must?

Titus

Do not heap odium on a hapless prince.
This is no time to break each other's hearts.
I have enough to madden and ensnare me
Without the tears of those beloved eyes.
No; let me hear those noble tones once more
That spoke to me so often of my duty.
I need it now. Stifle the voice of love.
Open your eyes to Reason and to Honour
1040 To make you see how cruel is my duty;
Stiffen my heart yourself against your charms,
And fight my weakness for me if you can.
Hold back the tears that will not be restrained,
Or, if our tears will not obey our will,
Let us calm sorrow with the thought of
                    Honour
And force the universe to recognise
Tears that a Roman Caesar and a Queen
May fitly shed. For part we must, Princess.

Berenice

Why tell me now? Or do you want to wound
                    me?
1050 What have you done? You let me think you
                    loved me,
You let me see you daily, till that pleasure

Was all I asked of life. You knew your laws
When first I told my love — what love you
know!
You could have said, "Poor foolish fated
woman,
Must you commit yourself, when hope is
none?
Why offer up a heart without a taker?"
Did you accept it only to return it,
When all my wish was to depend on you?
You know how many times they tried to stop
us;
1060 Then was the time: why could you not have
left me?
A thousand reasons could have eased my pain:
I could have seen your father as the man
Who caused my death — or else the crowd,
the Senate,
The State, the world, and not the one I loved.
I knew so long how much they hated me,
And so long had I waited for my doom —
A bitter doom I should not have received
Now that before me dawns a deathless joy,
Now that your love has won its liberty,
1070 Now Rome is silent and your father dead,
Now all the world is prostrate at your feet,
Now, in a word, there's only you to fear.

Titus   And no one but myself could bring me to it.
Then, I could tell myself the lies I liked;
I did not dare to look ahead and ask

What thing could come between us two and
                              part us.
I told myself my wishes must prevail;
I shut my eyes, trusted the impossible —
Or, no, I hoped to die before your eyes
1080 Rather than face the heartbreak of farewells.
Every new struggle only fed my flame.
The Empire spoke as one. But Honour's voice
Had never fallen yet upon my heart
In tones that sound on ears of Emperors.
I know the agonies that I must face;
I know too well I cannot live without you
And you will take my heart away with you;
But who cares if I live? For I must rule.

Berenice   Rule then, go on; appease the voice of
                              Honour;
1090 I shall not stop you. Only one thing kept me:
Simply to hear your voice, the self-same voice
After so many vows to love for ever,
Confess its perjuries before my face
And order me to leave your sight and go.
I wished to hear you say it. That is all.
I hear no more, and now farewell for ever.
— For ever! Oh, my lord, and have you
                              thought
How dreadful is that word for those that love?
A month from now, a year, shall we endure,
1100 My lord, that all those seas should come
                              between us,
That day should rise and day should fade to
                              night,

And never Titus see his Berenice
Nor I all day see Titus? — But enough;
I was deceived, I could have saved my pains.
This heartless lover is consoled already —
What will he care how long I am away?
Days endless for me will be short for him.

Titus I shall not have to count them. Ere long, I
       hope,
Snatches of mourning carried by report
1110 Will make you own that you were loved
       indeed;
You'll see that Titus could not survive the
       loss —

Berenice Well then, my lord, why do we have to part?
I speak no more of happiness in marriage:
But am I doomed by Rome never to see you?
May I not share with you the air you breathe?

Titus So be it then, my lady. Do not go.
I give you best. But, as I know myself,
I shall not cease to fight myself, and you;
I shall not cease from straying in the ways
1120 That lead me to your arms. And, more than
       that,
I know this moment that my rebel heart
Forgets its role, and only thinks of love.

Berenice What then, my lord, oh, what could happen
       then?
Do you think Rome is waiting to revolt?

Titus	And who knows how they'll take this latest
	insult?
	What if they talked, and talk should grow to
	murmurs,
	Murmurs to clamour — What am I to do?
	Must I defend my choice by spilling blood?
	If they do not, but try to sell their silence,
1130	What price will they exact, or what
	concessions
	Will they expect of me one day for this?
	Will there be anything they dare not ask?
	Can I maintain laws that I cannot keep?
Berenice	So you forget the tears of Berenice?
Titus	Forget your tears! How can you say such
	things?
Berenice	Will you for unjust laws that you could alter
	Condemn yourself to endless misery?
	Rome has her rights, my lord, but so have
	you.
	And are her claims more sacrosanct than
	yours?
1140	Come, speak.
Titus	You tear my heart in two!
Berenice	My lord, and you weep, and you are
	Emperor.
Titus	My lady, it is true. You see me in tears,

In grief, in horror. But when I took the
                              Empire
I had to swear to uphold the rights of Rome;
And so I must. For more than once, of old,
She has required this virtue in my peers.
Go back to her beginnings. You would see
                              them
Always devoted to her sovereign will;
One, jealous of his word, goes back to face
1150 Death in prompt torture at his enemies'
                              hands;
Another sends a victor son to die;
Another, dry of eye and careless-seeming,
Watches the death of sons that he has
                              doomed.
Unhappy men! But first in Roman hearts
Stood ever love of Rome and love of glory.
I know that Titus, if he lets you go,
Will top the bitterest effort history knows
And far surpass their pitch of sacrifice.
But after all, my lady, do you think me
1160 Unfit to leave the memory to my heirs
That all their pains can barely hope to rival?

Berenice   No, I am sure that anything is easy
To your barbarity; I think you fit
To take my life! Oh yes, I understand.
I am not asking you to let me stay —
I, stay? What, I? and ask to be the butt
Of crowds that hate me and will jeer at me?
I asked to see if you would dare refuse me.

You have, and soon you will not need to fear
me.
1170 Oh, I'll not hurl invective at your head
Nor pray for penalties on broken vows:
If Heaven has any pity for me still
My last request will be, to be forgotten;
And all the vengeance, dying, I bequeath
Shall be the memories rankling in your breast:
Such love, I know, can never be effaced;
That the pain I suffer and the joys you took,
These, and the blood that here I mean to
spill,
Are torturers I leave to work behind me —
1180 I am not sorry for my constancy —
But that is all the justice I desire.
Farewell.

[Exit Berenice. Enter Paulinus]

Scene 6

Paulinus   What was she going out to do?
Is she prepared to leave at last?

Titus   Oh, Paulinus,
This is the end; it is the end for me!
The Queen intends to die. Come, we must
follow her.
Hurry, she needs our help.

Paulinus   Have you forgotten

~ 60 ~

Your orders that she should be closely
                                        followed?
Her women, ever watchful in her service,
Will quickly turn her from her thoughts of
                                        death.
1190 No, no, all will be well. The worst is done.
Only go on, my lord. The day is yours.
I know you could not hear her without pity;
No more could I endure to see her suffer.
But think of the future; think of the applause.
The rank of glory —

Titus   No, I am a savage.
I loathe myself. Nero, the hated Nero,
Never brought cruelty to such a height.
But Berenice shall not die; I'll save her.
Come; Rome will say whatever Rome may
                                        say.

Paulinus   1200 My lord!

Titus   I don't know what I'm saying,
                                        Paulinus,
The weight of grief has overpowered my
                                        mind.

Paulinus   Do nothing to disturb your growing fame.
The news is out already of your parting,
And Rome has turned to triumph from
                                        dismay:
Each temple steams in honour of your name;
The people, with your praises on their lips,

~ 61 ~

Stream everywhere with bays to deck your
statues.

Titus   Oh Rome! Oh Berenice! Wretched me!
Must I be Emperor, and love?

[Enter Antiochus]

Scene 7

Antiochus   My lord,
1210 What have you done? Our fair Berenice
Must now be dying in her woman's arms,
Deaf to all tears, deaf to all counsellors.
She cries aloud for poison or a knife.
Your name is all that holds her from her
death.
Her glance is always turned towards your
chambers;
She calls for you. I cannot bear to watch.
Will you not let her see your face again?
Save so much virtue, so much grace and
beauty,
Or show, my lord, you lack a human heart;
1220 Give her one word!

Titus   Tell me what word. Ah
Heaven!
Am I as much as living at this hour?

[Enter Rutilus]

Scene 8

Rutilus My lord, the Senate, the Consuls and the
Tribunes
Come to seek audience in the name of Rome,
Great crowds are with them, thronging your
apartment
And waiting with impatience for your coming.

Titus This is your voice, great Gods! It comes to
steel
A heart you see about to break away.

Paulinus Come then, my lord, pass into the next
chamber
And see the Senate.

Antiochus   Oh quickly, to the Queen!

Paulinus 1230 Could you, my lord, put such a grievous slight
Upon the imperial dignity of Rome?

Titus No. All is well, Paulinus. We will see them.
I cannot shirk this duty if I would.
Prince, go and see the Queen. When I return
She'll have no cause to put my love in doubt.

[Exeunt]

Act V

Scene 1

Arbaces [solus]

Arbaces Where shall I find this over-amorous prince?
Heaven grant it's not too late for me to give
       him
The news I am sure he never hoped to hear!

[Enter Antiochus]

Scene 2

Back at a lucky hour, my lord, indeed!

Antiochus 1240 I don't know why it pleases you so much,
Arbaces. All that it brought me was despair.

Arbaces The Queen, my lord, is sailing.

Antiochus   Sailing?

Arbaces   Now,
          This very night. Her order's given. She is hurt
          That Titus left her in her grief too long.
          It is not fury now, but proud resentment,
          In which she gives up Rome, and its Emperor,
          And even plans to sail before the city
          Can get the news and celebrate her going.
          She leaves a word for Caesar.

Antiochus   Incredible,
     1250 Great Gods! And Titus?

Arbaces   Titus I did not see.
          He is beset by a rejoicing crowd
          That cheers the titles which the Senate gives
                              him —
          Titles, cheers, honours, each one a com-
                              mitment
          Stronger than any love, or all her tears,
          To force his wavering will the way of duty.
          The thing is done: they may not meet again.

Antiochus   Plentiful grounds for hope, in truth, Arbaces;
          But Fortune has so cruelly played with me
          That everything you tell me makes me
                              tremble
     1260 To anger her if I so much as hope —
          But what is this? Titus is coming back;
          What can he want?

                    [Enter Titus]

Scene 3

Titus
[to his
followers]

Stay here, and do not follow.
So, Prince, I come at last to keep my promise;
My heart, my thoughts, are full of Berenice;
Her tears, and yours, have pierced me to the
quick.
And I must heal a grief less deep than mine.
So come, Prince, come; I'll have you see
yourself,
For the last time, whether I love or no.

[Exit Titus]

Scene 4

Antiochus

Well, so much for the new-born hope you gave me!
1270 And so much for the triumph that you
promised!
The Queen had taken umbrage and was
sailing?
Titus had left her, they would meet no more?
What have I done, great Gods, to earn the chain
Of linked misfortunes blasting all my days?
Each moment of my life has seen me whirled
From fear to hope, from hope to mad despair;
And still I live? — Titus! Berenice!
Dread Gods, you shall not mock my tears
again!

[Exeunt Antiochus and Arbaces. Enter Titus and Berenice]

Scene 5

Berenice	No, I am not listening. My mind's made up.
	1280 I want to leave. Why did you want to see me?
	Why come to make it even worse for me?
	You should be pleased: I do not want to see
	you.
Titus	But let me speak, I beg.
Berenice	The time is past.
Titus	One word, my lady!
Berenice	No.
Titus	She drives me wild.
	What means, Princess, this sudden change of
	mind?
Berenice	The thing is done. You want me gone
	tomorrow.
	And I have settled that I go today;
	And I am going.
Titus	Wait.
Berenice	False lover, wait?
	Why should I wait? To hear a jeering crowd
	1290 Make my misfortune echo through the city
	Cannot you hear it now, this savage joy
	Against one single woman lost in tears?

~ 68 ~

	What do they hold against me? What have I
	done?
	Nothing, alas, but loving you too well.

Titus   But do you listen to a crowd in a fury?

Berenice   Everything here is hateful to my sight —
These chambers you had planned and built
        for me,
Whose walls sheltered my love these many
        years
And seemed to prove your lasting love for me,
1300 Walls that confront me with so many
        emblems
That intertwine our names each with the other —
All lying prophets that I cannot bear —
Come on, Phenice.

Titus   Gods! but how unjust!

Berenice   Go back, go back to your majestic Senate
Which comes to praise you for your cruelty!
Did you find pleasure in their eulogies?
Are you entirely happy with your glory?
Have you agreed my name shall be forgotten?
Or, as a fuller penance for your love,
1310 Have you agreed that you will always hate me?

Titus   No, I have made no promise! Could I hate you?
Could I dismiss all thought of Berenice?
But what a time to choose, great Gods! to
        level

Such cruel and baseless accusations on me!
You do not know me. Go back these five
                              years
And reckon all the moments, count the days
Of my most wild and most tempestuous
                              passion.
Nothing was like today. Never, I swear,
Have you been loved as ardently as now,
1320 Never —

Berenice   You love me, or you say as much.
And yet I go, and you will have it so.
What, can you get such rapture from my
                              grief?
Or fear to see the fount of tears run dry?
What use to me was the change of heart?
Ah, show some pity, let me see less love;
Let me at least think as I sail away
That I had long been banished from your
                              heart
And that you let me go without regret.

[Titus seizes a letter and reads it]

That is the letter that I wrote for you;
1330 It tells you all I ask from your affection.
Read it, deceiver, read and let me go.

Titus   You shall not go! No, I will not allow it.
What? then this departure was a trick:
You want to die? and leave, of all I love,
Only a sorrowful memory behind?

— Send for Antiochus! Someone bring him
here!

[Exit Phenice]

Scene 6

[Berenice falls back upon a seat]

Titus   The tale that I must tell you is the truth,
My lady. Once I knew a dreadful day
Would come when duty with its stern
constraint
1340 Would force me to relinquish you for ever,
I schooled my soul against that dire farewell,
Rehearsed my pains, my fears, your tears,
your outcries,
And thought myself well armed against the
blows
That even the heaviest hardships could inflict;
Yet fear what I might, I must confess
That I had not foreseen the half of them.
I thought my will was stronger to resist,
And I am shamed that I should falter so.
The whole of Rome was ranged before my
face,
1350 The Senate spoke. I could not bring myself
To attend to what I heard, and their rejoicing
Brought nothing but a blank and chilling
silence.
Rome is still ignorant how you will fare;

And I myself pause at each step to wonder
If I am Emperor or Roman still.
I came to you not knowing why I came,
Drawn by my love or, as I think, perhaps
Hoping to learn my nature and its needs.
What do I find? Your eyes are full of death;
1360 I find you are escaping me, to die.
It is too much: at sight of this, my grief
Has reached the limit of my power to feel it.
It seems that I have nothing left to suffer;
But I have seen a pathway of escape —
Do not suppose that you have worn me down
To offer you the wedding of your dreams.
Sore as were the straits you placed me in
Honour assails me unremittingly,
Reminding me that your husband cannot be
1370 The Emperor of Rome, and, after all
My shifts and struggles, even less than ever.
And less, far less, my lady, may I offer
To give up the Empire, and with you
                              withdraw,
Proud of my bonds, too happy in my love,
Out past the known bounds of the universe.
Why, you would blush for shame at such a
                              lover,
And shrink to countenance a follower,
A so-called Emperor stripped of his Empire,
Without a court, a dreadful monument
1380 Of how love can emasculate a man.
There is a way, you know, a nobler way
To rise above the torments that beset me,
A way that I have studied in the record

Of many a hero and of many a Roman,
Who, tired of meeting countless blows of fate,
Have all considered this insistency
As a coded order to give up the struggle.
So now, my lady, if I have to see you
Always in tears, and still resolved to die;
1390 If I must always tremble for your days;
If you refuse to swear that you will live —
My lady, you have other tears to shed;
For as I am, I could do anything,
And it may be that here, before your eyes,
My blood will stain the last of our farewells.

Berenice   Alas!

Titus   No, nothing is too difficult,
And on your choice depends my death or life.
Consider all, if I am dear to you.

[Enter Antiochus]

Scene 7

Ah, Prince, I wanted you. Come in and be
1400 Witness of all the weakness I have shown;
Tell me if this is lack of love indeed:
Decide between us.

Antiochus   Oh, I believe, I know you;
But this unhappy Prince you do not know.

You honoured me, my lord, with your
esteem —
A prize for which (I can admit it now)
I vied with all your friends, and paid my
blood
To buy it if I could; thus, now, you have
Told me unasked the story of your loves,
The Queen of hers, and you, my lord, of
yours.
1410 — The Queen may disavow me if she will. —
She found me always ready to applaud you,
Eager to serve her and deserve your trust.
You may suppose you owe me thanks for this;
But could you guess that this devoted friend
Concealed a rival?

Titus   What?

Antiochus   You had to know
at last.
My lord, I've always worshipped Berenice;
I've tried to stifle love, and always failed;
But what I could not help, I did disguise.
Of late, the feeble hope that you must yield
1420 Brought me a flattering semblance of relief.
The Queen's dismay extinguished it again,
And all those tears, which only called for
you.
I came myself, my lord, to bring you back.
And you returned; you love, and you are
loved.
You yielded, as I knew full well you would.

Now for the last time I've reviewed my fate,
Questioned my heart to find what it will bear
And called up reason in its full array;
Never has love burned stronger in my breast.
1430 It takes more force than mine to burst these
bonds;
Only in death will they be overcome.
So I shall die. I wanted you to know.
Yes, it was I who brought him back, my
lady,
I was successful, nor do I regret.
I pray the Gods to pour on both your heads
Unnumbered blessings in an endless chain —
Or if they hoard some residue of wrath
Let them divert it from that precious life,
Transferring all the fury of their justice
1440 On these doomed days I dedicate to you.

Berenice
[rising]   No more, no more! Your noble words, my
lords,
Are more than generous, but they torture me!
I look on you or turn to him, and see
Only the lineaments of despair and grief,
Hear only of torments, blood about to flow.
[to Titus]   You, my lord, know my heart, and well you
know
You never saw me hanker for the Empire —
Not all the power of Rome, nor all the purple
The Caesars wear ever seduced my eyes;
1450 I was in love — in love — and craved for
love.
Today, I do confess I felt one pang.

I thought your love for me was running dry.
I was mistaken, and you love me still;
I saw you moved, I saw the tears you shed.
But Berenice must not cost you this,
Nor must you, now that all hearts turn to
Titus,
Bereave them of their darling joy and hope.
I think, in these five years until today,
That you could look to me for love unfeigned;
1460 Nor is this all: in this our darkest moment
I mean to make my sacrifice complete —
I will live on, obedient to your word;
Farewell, my lord, and rule. We meet no
more.

[to Antiochus] Prince, after that farewell, you surely see
I cannot think of leaving him I love
To let another woo me far from Rome.
Live on, and make the effort heroes can;
Take for your models Titus and myself:
Titus loves me, and forces me to leave,
1470 And I love Titus, so I shall obey.
Let me hear no more talk of pains and
prisons;
Farewell; and let all three of us bequeath
The example of the fondest, cruellest love
That men have known, to pity or admire.
— They are ready. Let me leave. No, do not
come.

[to Titus] For the last time, my lord, farewell.

[Exit]

Antiochus   Oh pity!

[*Exit*]

NOTES

Notes to the Preface refer to the superscript numbers in the text; notes to the play refer to line numbers. The notes and translation of the Preface are the editor's.

Preface

1   The quotation, in which Racine combines two separated phrases, comes from Suetonius, *Life of Titus*, vii. As he quotes it in Latin, the sentence omits what Racine translates as 'who passionately loved Berenice'.

2   Virgil, *Aeneid*, iv.

3   This sentence seems to give the lie to those commentators who suggest that Berenice was Titus's mistress in the play, though she was in history.

4   *Ars poetica*, l. 23.

5   Aristotle's *anagnorisis*: recognition of the truth.

6   The plots of seventeenth-century French tragedy were complex, derived from the succession of dramatic surprises characteristic of those of tragi-comedy.

7   In the prologue of his first play, *Andria*, Terence admits to combining the matter of two of Menander's comedies in creating his own.

8   Verisimilitude is the fundamental concept of the so-called

classical system of French tragedy. The argument developed here is a counterblast against those of Corneille's tragedies, particularly the later ones, whose plots are complex and whose characters often behave in an exceptional, almost superhuman heroic manner.

9 Implicit here is the contrast with the reception given to Corneille's *Tite et Bérénice* which was no great box-office success.

10 The same emphasis had been expressed in Molière's *La Critique de L'Ecole des Femmes* (scene vi) in 1663, and would be found again in Boileau's *Art poétique* (iii, l. 25) in 1674.

11 Racine alludes to the *Critique de Bérénice*, by Abbé Montfaucon de Villars, a captious, Cornelian pamphlet published in January 1671. The dramatist's irritation and love of irony led him to misquote and distort part of Villars's argument.

12 The four parts of tragedy are, in order: exposition (*protasis*); 'thickening' of the plot (*epitasis*: French, *le noeud*); peripety (*catastesis*: reversal); denouement (*catastrophe*).

13 Racine refers scornfully to Villars's ironical remarks about the number of times the characters say '*hélas!*' (27 in all, including the very last word of the play), and to his mock-deference to the rules.

Berenice

70   *Ostia*: the port of Rome, at the mouth of the river Tiber. Imminent departure and its frustration reflect several times the conflict between hope and fear.

98-112   This passage refers to the Jewish revolt which began in AD 66, and to the siege of Jerusalem which ended four years later. Arbaces' recollections are drawn from the account by Josephus (*Wars of the Jews*, V, xi, 3).

162-4 The apotheosis of the late emperor was a ceremony introduced in 42 BC, when Julius Caesar was raised to divine status.

174 Like Antiochus, Berenice seems almost certain that Titus will marry her.

189 *Agrippa*: he became tetrach of Northern Palestine in AD 51.

192 An echo of Julius Caesar's celebrated phrase: '*Veni, vidi, vici*' ('I came, I saw, I conquered').

231 In fact, Berenice did not go to Rome until AD 75, four years after Titus's return there on the death of his father, Vespasian.

233 *Caesarea*: Palestinae or Philippi? Berenice had lived in both cities.

256-82 These speeches reveal the self-absorption of both characters, and their insensitivity to each other's deepest feelings. Berenice does not even respond to Antiochus's word of farewell. See also Berenice's indifference to Phenice's reproach (ll. 282-7).

289-96 The political reality which forms the crux of the action. Berenice's speech which follows shows her carried away by her passion into a certainty and pride (*hubris*) which will be destroyed by that reality.

349 The vices of Nero (Emperor AD 54-68) had been condoned by many who wished to curry favour with him. Titus repudiates him (see Paulinus's comment, l. 343) and will in the end uphold the true traditions of Rome, hostile to marriages with foreigners and royalty (ll. 416-83).

382-90 Cleopatra in fact lived in Rome openly as Julius

Caesar's mistress until his assassination in 44 BC. Later, she became Mark Antony's mistress. Octavian (the Emperor Augustus from 27 BC) defeated the forces of Antony and Cleopatra in the battle of Actium (31 BC).

391 *Caligula*: Emperor, AD 37-41, notorious for his cruelty.

398-401 Pallas was a freedman of the Emperor Claudius; Felix was the husband of three queens: the two referred to here were the granddaughter of Antony and Cleopatra and the sister of Berenice.

421-3 In AD 70 Vespasian was proclaimed emperor by his troops in revolt against Vitellius when he was commanding the armies in the east. The short reign of Vitellius, like those of Galba and Otho before him, had been marked by civil war.

495-6 Berenice's good influence on Titus is not attested by the historians: quite the contrary in fact. See also l. 512.

600-01 This is historically correct. Berenice had been insulted and reviled by the Romans. See also ll. 1166-7.

623-58 Like so many of Racine's characters, Berenice deludes herself, only to find eventually the inescapable hard truth.

681-4 These lines refer to the triumph accorded to Titus and Vespasian in AD 71 for their victory over the Jews. The procession of triumphal chariots, legionaries carrying the spoils of war, and prisoners ended on the Capitol, at the temple of Jupiter.

746-50 Unconscious irony: Titus reigned for only just over two years.

840-3 Berenice is unable to conceal her disappointment at finding Antiochus, not Titus.

867 In spite of wilful self-deception, Berenice does need to

find the truth: she will do so in the final recognition. See also ll. 883, 900.

1027 Berenice's impetuous entrance cuts short Titus's great soliloquy: contrast l. 550. The scene which follows is the dramatic centre of the play.

1136-9 The Oriental monarch's incomprehension of the force of Roman anti-despotic tradition prompts Titus's reassertion of it and his submission to it (ll. 1142-5). He cites three extreme instances of Romans bowing to it: Atilius Regulus (l. 1149) was tortured and killed by the Carthaginians in 250 BC because he would not, as they demanded, advise the Romans to accept their peace proposals; Manlius Torquatus (l. 1151) ordered his son to be executed (340 BC) for disobeying a consul's edict; Lucius Junius Brutus, consul in 509 BC, put his own two sons to death for attempting to restore the dynasty of the Tarquins (ll. 1152-3).

1234-5 The ambiguity of these lines creates suspense as the final phase of the drama unfolds.

1267-8 Antiochus, assuming that Titus and Berenice are about to be reconciled, does not follow the Emperor into her apartment.

1277-8 Antiochus sees Titus and Berenice coming out of her apartment; believing them to be reconciled, he beats a hasty retreat.

1300-01 Berenice refers to the garlands surrounding her initial and that of Titus with which the room is decorated.

1329 According to Louis Racine (*Mémoires sur la vie et les ouvrages de Jean Racine*, 1747), at the first performance Titus snatched the letter from Berenice as she made her entrance, and read it aloud. This was criticized: in all subsequent performances Titus reads the letter in silence.

1381-7 Titus has in mind the noble suicides of mythological heroes like Hercules (who flung himself on a funeral pyre to end the agony when he put on the poisoned shirt of Nessus) and Roman heroes like Cato (who committed suicide rather than submit to Caesar when the Pompeians were defeated at Thapsus, 46 BC) and Brutus (who took his own life after the Pompeians were defeated at Philippi, 42 BC). Both Antiochus and Berenice also threaten suicide; but noble, dignified resignation prevails in the closing lines of the play (ll. 1455-70).

1448-9 Part of the truth Berenice has discovered is revealed in the contrast between these lines and ll. 293-303.

1453 The *anagnorisis*, Berenice's moment of recognition.

1469-70 A paraphrase of the words of Suetonius quoted at the head of the Preface.